THE NATURE KIDS GUIDE TO

BISON

DAVID ANDERSON

LP Media Inc. Publishing
Text copyright © 2026 by LP Media Inc.
All rights reserved.

For information address LP Media Inc. Publishing,
30012 Variolite St NW, Princeton MN 55371
www.lpmedia.org

Publication Data

Bison
The Nature Kid's Guide to Bison — First edition.

Summary: "Learn all about Bison, the Nature Kid Way"
— Provided by publisher.

ISBN: 979-8-89818-153-6

[1. Bison – Non-Fiction] I. Title.

Title: The Nature Kid's Guide to Bison

CONTENTS

PRAIRIE PARADISE

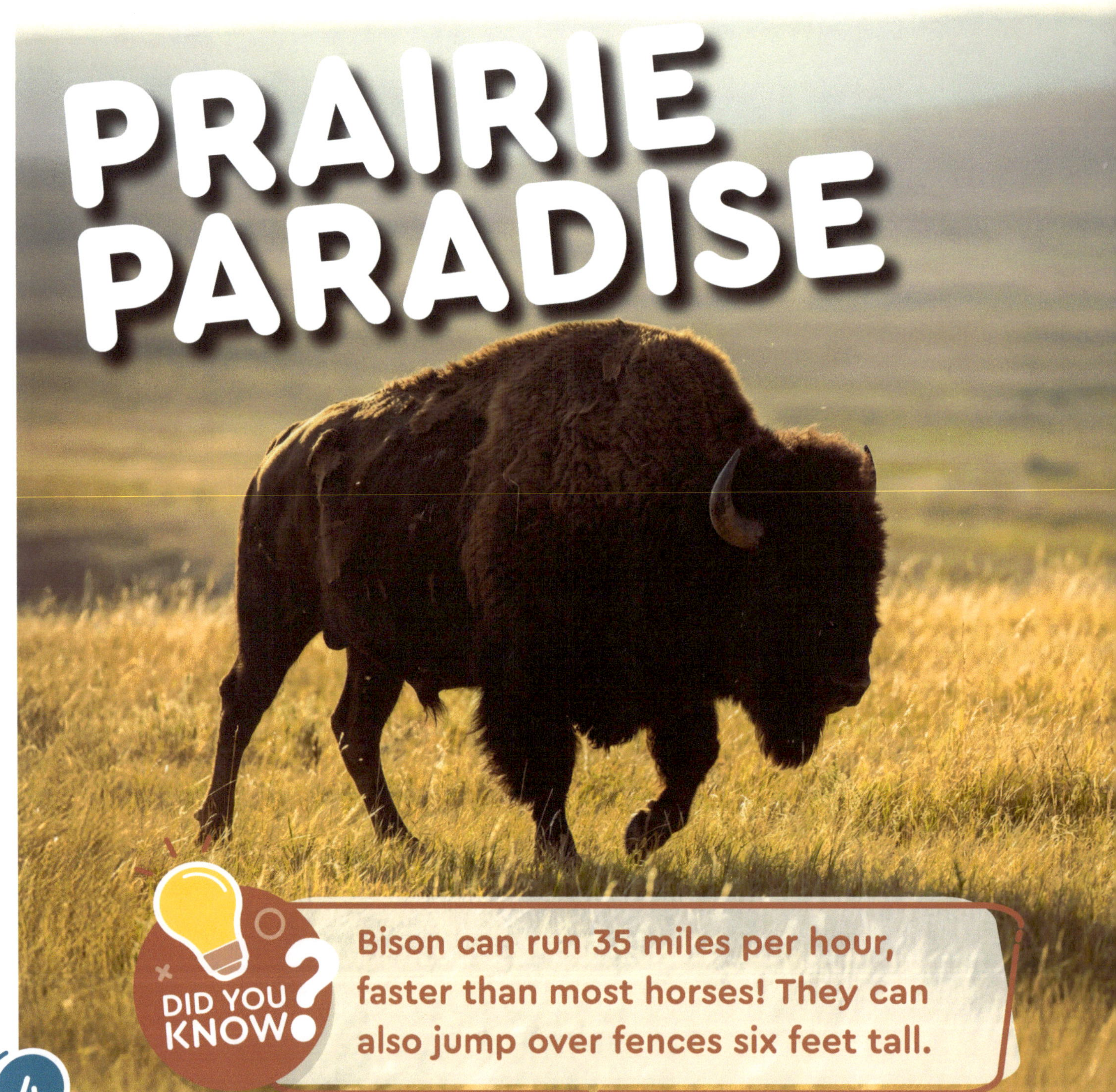

Snort! A bison lifts its shaggy head. All around, grass stretches for miles.

Bison live on **prairies**. Prairies are flat, grassy lands. These open spaces stretch across North America. This is where bison make their home.

Prairies have hot summers and cold winters. Bison handle both well. Their thick fur keeps them warm. In summer, they shed extra fur.

Bison need lots of grass to eat. Prairies have plenty! These grasslands also have rivers and streams. Bison need to drink water every day.

Most bison live in protected parks today. Yellowstone National Park has wild bison that roam free.

BISON BOUND

Thump! Heavy hooves cross wide open land. A herd moves on.

Bison once roamed across most of North America. They lived from Canada down to Mexico. Millions walked migrated across the prairie.

Today, there are far fewer bison. Most stay on private ranches or parks. They still need big spaces to graze.

Wild bison **herds** move would with the seasons. They travel far to find fresh grass.

Baby bison are called 'red dogs' for their orange-red fur. They can walk just hours after birth!

BIG BEASTS

Rumble! A huge bison stands tall. It towers over the horse

Bison are the largest land animals in North America. A male can weigh up to 2,000 pounds. That is as heavy as a small car!

Males are bigger than females. Females weigh about half as much. Both have large, heavy heads.

Male bison stand about 6 feet tall at the shoulder. Their bodies can be 11 feet long. These big bodies need lots of food.

A bison's head alone can weigh over 50 pounds. That is heavier than most dogs!

BUILT BEEFY

DID YOU KNOW?
Bison have 14 pairs of ribs – more than humans! These extra ribs protect their huge lungs.

Grunt! A bison shakes dust from its coat. Muscles ripple underneath.

Bison have strong, powerful bodies. Their front legs are thick and sturdy, with big muscles that help them push through deep snow.

A bison's hump is made of muscle. This hump sits above the shoulders and helps the head swing side to side. Bison use this motion to clear snow and find grass.

Their bones are heavy and dense. Strong leg bones hold up all that weight. These tough bodies are perfectly built for prairie life.

SUPER SNIFFERS

Sniff! A bison lifts its nose high. It smells the wind.

Bison have an excellent sense of smell. They can detect scents from over 2 miles away. Their large noses help them find the freshest grass, even under snow!

Their noses also keep them safe. Bison can smell wolves and other predators before they get close.

This is important because bison have poor eyesight.

Bison can even sense a storm coming from many miles away using their nose!

HORNS HELP

Crack! Two bison slam horns together. The sound echoes across the prairie.

Both male and female bison have horns. These curved, sharp horns grow directly above each eye.

Bison use their horns to protect themselves. A quick jab can hurt a wolf or coyote. Even bears stay away from angry bison.

Over time, horns can grow up to 2 feet long. They are made of bone covered with a hard shell. Unlike antlers, bison horns never fall off, they keep them for life.

Bison horns start growing when calves are just months old. They keep growing their whole life!

GRASS GRAZERS

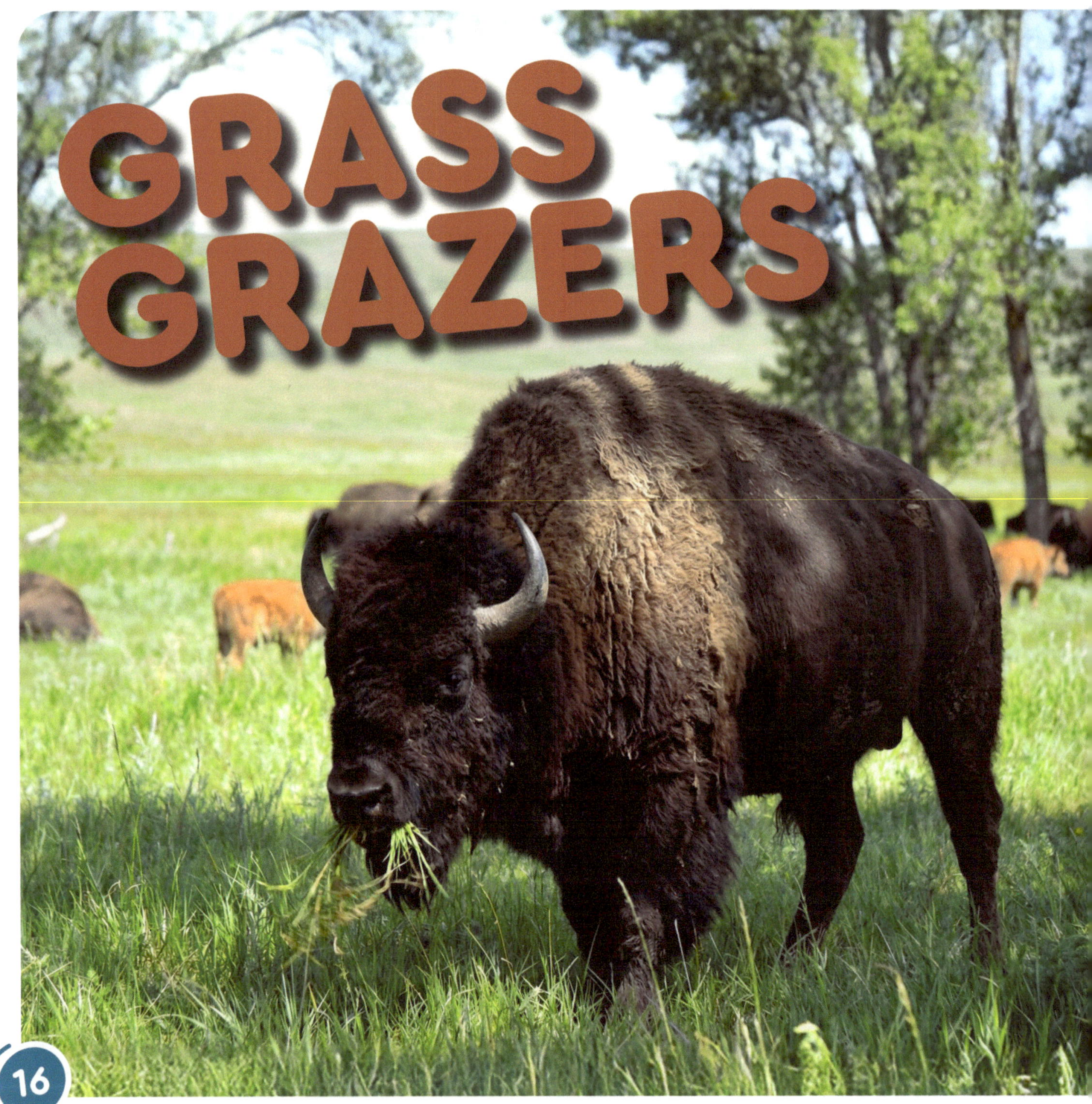

Chomp! A bison bites off a mouthful of grass. It chews slowly.

Bison eat mostly grass. They spend many hours each day **grazing** on prairies and meadows. Their wide mouths help them take big bites.

Bison also eat other plants. They munch on shrubs, twigs, and weeds. In winter, they eat dried grasses hidden under snow.

A bison can eat up to 30 pounds of food each day. Their big stomachs break down all those tough plants.

Bison have four stomach parts to digest grass. So do cows!

GRUNT TALK

FUN FACT!
Bison can make sounds that are very loud, even louder than a lawn mower!

Bellow! A bison calls out loudly. Others turn to listen.

Bison make many sounds to talk to each other. They grunt, snort, and bellow. Each sound means something different.

Males bellow loudly during summer to tell others they are nearby. This deep call can be heard from 3 miles away!

Mothers and calves use softer sounds. A quiet grunt helps them stay close in the herd. Calves also bleat when they need their mothers.

Bison use body language too. A raised tail means danger is near. Pawing the ground shows anger.

WATCH OUT

Howl! A wolf pack sees a bison herd. They watch. They wait.

Bison face danger from very few predators. Wolves are their main threat. A wolf pack works as a team to chase bison.

Grizzly bears hunt bison too. They look for weak or young ones. Mountain lions can also hunt bison. They will usually only attack calves.

Healthy adult bison are hard to catch. They are big and fast. Most predators stay away. Wolves catch fewer than one in ten bison they chase.

Coyotes may attack bison calves that wander too far from the herd.

CIRCLE STRONG

Stomp! Bison form a tight circle. Calves stand safely in the middle.

Bison stay safe by sticking together. When danger comes, adults form a wall around the young. Their big bodies block predators.

Adult bison face outward in a circle. Sharp horns point at any threat. This makes it hard for wolves to reach calves.

Bison can also sprint up to 35 miles per hour. This helps them escape when they are attacked.

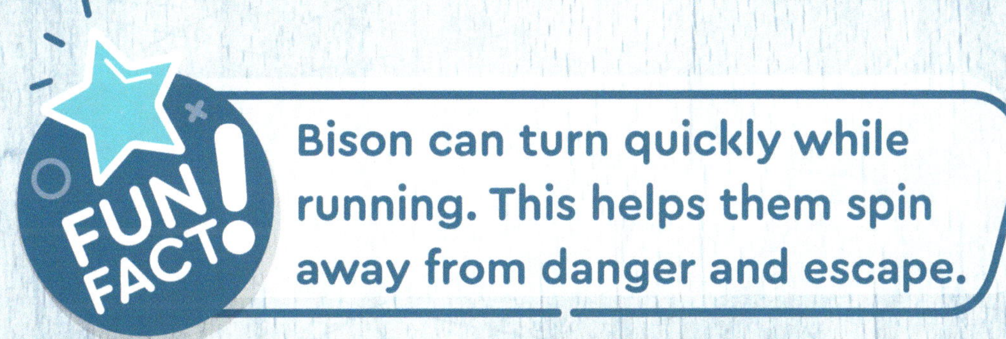

Bison can turn quickly while running. This helps them spin away from danger and escape.

23

24

Whoosh! A bison herd races across the plains. Dust flies everywhere.

Bison can run up to 40 miles per hour. Their powerful legs carry their heavy bodies fast.

Bison walk many miles each day. Herds travel to find fresh grass and water. Wild bison follow the same paths year after year.

In winter, bison swing their huge heads to clear snow and find food. Their strong necks are like built-in show shovels!

Bison hooves act like snowshoes. Their wide, split hooves help them walk on snow.

DAILY ROUTINE

Rustle! A bison herd walks the prairie looking for breakfast.

Bison spend nine to eleven hours a day eating. Early morning and late afternoon are their busiest feeding times.

Bison rest during the hottest part of the day. They lie down to chew their cud. This helps them digest tough grass.

Bison also love to roll in dirt. These dusty spots are called **wallows**. Rolling helps remove bugs and loose fur.

Bison wallows can be over ten feet wide. Some have even been used for thousands of years!

HERD HANGOUT

Grunt! Bison gather in a big group. They eat grass together.

Bison live in groups called herds. Some herds have about 20 bison. Other herds have more than 1,000!

Female bison stay with their calves. They are together all year.

Male bison often make smaller groups. But they join the big herd during mating season.

Herds find food together. Herds help bison stay safe too.

One bison herd stretched for 25 miles! It crossed the Great Plains of North America.

29

BELLOW BATTLES

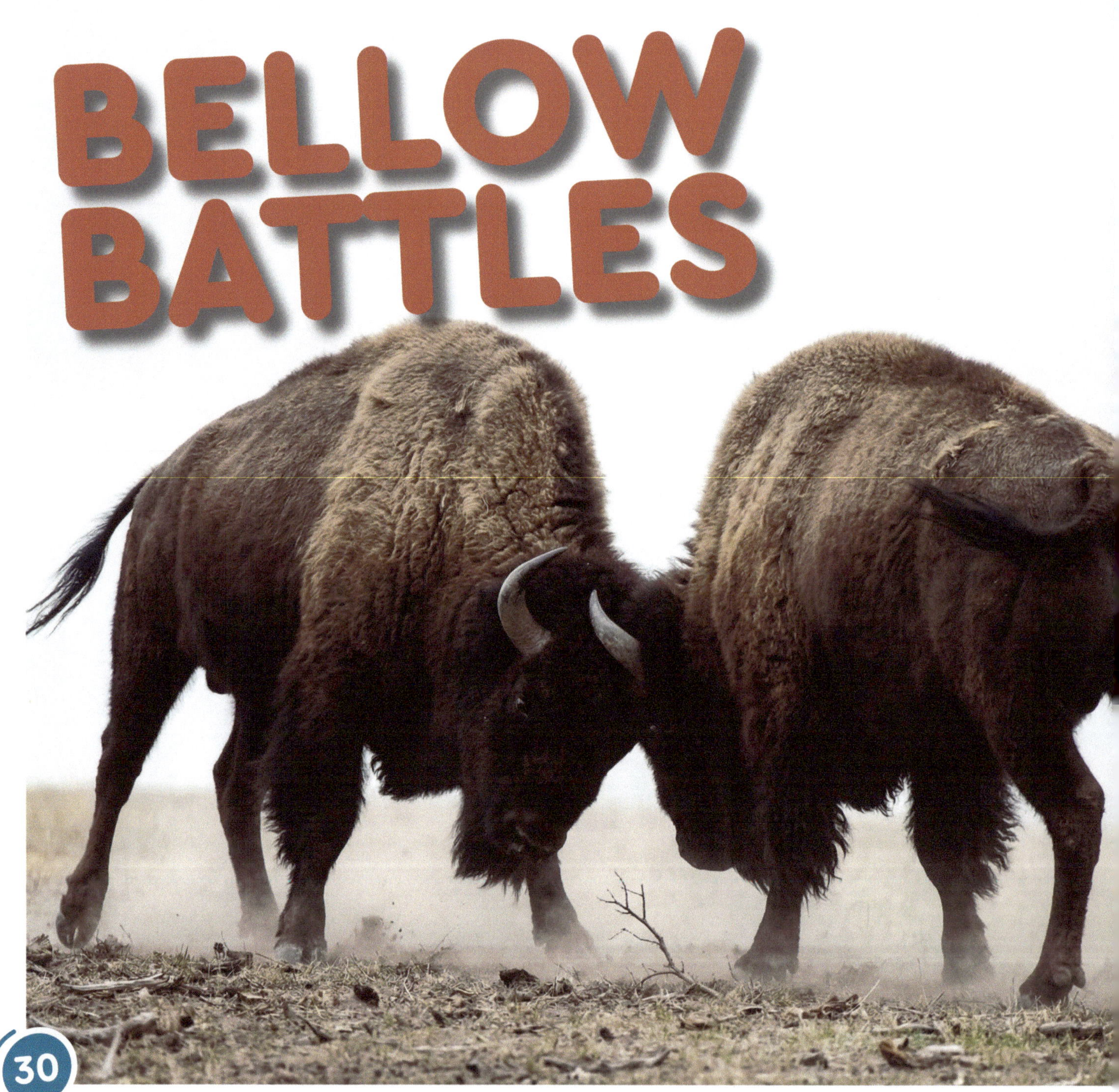

Thunder! Two big male bison face off. Their hooves shake the ground.

Male bison compete for mates in summer. They make deep bellowing sounds that can be heard from far away.

Males show off their size by walking stiffly and pawing the ground. Sometimes they even charge at each other.

All this fighting is worth it. The winner gets to lead the herd. The loser has to try to find another herd to lead.

Male bison lose up to 200 pounds during mating season because they are too busy competing to eat!

CUTE CALVES

DID YOU KNOW?
Mother bison recognize their calves by smell. Each calf has a unique scent that helps mom find her baby!

Hurry! A baby bison runs back to the herd. It was too busy playing to realize they left!

Baby bison are called **calves**. These little ones are born in spring. Newborn calves weigh about 30 to 70 pounds.

Calves have reddish-orange fur. This bright color helps mothers spot them in the herd. The fur turns brown after a few months.

Calves can stand within 30 minutes of being born. They start walking soon after that. Within hours, they can run with the herd.

MOM
KNOWS

Grunt! A mother bison snorts at a coyote. She guards her calf.

Mother bison take care of their calves for about one year. They nurse their babies with rich milk. This helps calves grow strong and healthy.

Mothers stay very close to their young. They use their big bodies to block danger. A mother will charge at any animal that gets too close.

Calves learn by watching their mothers. They copy how to find water and good grass. Mothers teach their calves how to survive in the wild.

Mother bison sometimes adopt orphaned calves from their herd.

ALMOST
GONE

Snap! A lone buffalo walks across the frozen ground. Millions used to roam these plains.

Long ago, 30 million bison lived in North America. Hunters killed most of them in the 1800s. By 1889, fewer than 1,000 bison were left.

Why did this happen? People wanted bison hides. They made leather from the hides. They also cleared land. They made room for farms. They made room for railroads.

Bison almost disappeared forever.

Hunters once killed over 5,000 bison in one day. Millions were wiped out in just a few decades.

BOUNCING BACK

Click! A park ranger counts bison. The herd is growing!

People worked hard to save bison. In the early 1900s, zoos helped. Ranches helped too. They kept the last herds safe. They helped bison have babies.

Today, about 500,000 bison live in North America. Many live in national parks. Yellowstone has a famous wild herd.

Bison show us something big. People can help animals come back!

In 1905, the Bronx Zoo sent 15 bison to Oklahoma. They started a new wild herd there!

GLOSSARY

prairies
Flat, grassy lands that stretch for miles and miles.

herd
A big group of animals that live and travel together.

grazing
Eating grass and plants by biting them off the ground.

wallows
Dusty spots in the dirt where bison roll around.

calves
Baby bison.